[handwritten inscription: To Hettie, Thanks [illegible signature]]

Roses Beneath My Wings

Elizabeth Billups

 FriesenPress

One Printers Way
Altona, MB R0G 0B0
Canada

www.friesenpress.com

ISBN
978-1-5255-8782-5 (Hardcover)
978-1-5255-8781-8 (Paperback)
978-1-5255-8783-2 (eBook)

1. POETRY, SUBJECTS & THEMES, WOMEN AUTHORS

Distributed to the trade by The Ingram Book Company

DEDICATION

This poem is dedicated to my dyslexic son, (Doors were closed) who has now achieved his life golds? When he was little, he asked me why everyone was closing the doors on him. As a mother, I encourage my son to put God first. Don't give up; God will see you through the difficult times. He has an infectious personality. I am proud of my son.

This is dedicated to all those who have experienced dyslexia and felt a lack of motivation but were given a chance and succeeded in life.

A Lonely Song

They closed the books on me, so many years ago. I sing the truth you see, please remember me. I am an old lonely song, please think about me. I am an old lonely song; will you please sing me!

The Royal Telephone

Devil Leave Me

The devil came today, to get me to sin and grin. Come with me today so we can sin and grin. Oh no, you devil! Get away from me!

I need no sin; I need no grin; because Jesus is my friend.

King James Version (KJV)
James 2:19 Thou believest that there is one God; thou doest well: the devils also believe, and tremble.

It's My Master's Will

The Lord touched me to say wake my child and travel this highway again; It's my master's will. Oh Lord, I am in so much pain, for this day shall be the same. My Lord no one stopped, by today to lend a helping hand. But why despair for it's my master's will.

Bless me today; Oh Lord keep me away from sin and shame, help me endure this day for this day shall be the same, for it's my master's will. Trouble and burdens are oh so hard to bear, but remember Jesus is always near; for it's my master's will.

King James Version (KJV)
Matthew 6:10 Thy kingdom come. Thy will be done in earth, as it is in heaven.

Doors Were Closed

Everywhere I turned they closed the doors on me. When I was in school, I tried to learn, my teachers became hostile. Oh, what a way to be. I did not know what was wrong, they closed the doors on me. I went to college to achieve my goals, and improve my life.

They closed the doors on me, what a way to be! I went to work. The managers yelled at me all the time, every day.

They closed the doors; everywhere I turned they closed the doors on me. I never gave up you see. Now I am an entrepreneur, these doors were not closed for me. Because you closed the doors, on me, my doors have open wide now can't you see.

King James Version (KJV)
Psalms 18: 2 The LORD is my rock, and my fortress, and my deliverer; my God, my strength, in whom I will trust; my buckler, and the horn of my salvation, and my high tower.

Alabama Snow

Alabama, snow comes once in a while; it's beautiful to see, it will make you smile. Alabama, snow makes you slip and slide.

You be scared to drive; it will make you stay home inside. Alabama, snow makes the school close down; So, children can run, and play in the streets, in Alabama, snow! Alabama, snow can be seen so far and near; It will make you want some more. Alabama, snow Doesn't last very long; for you and me. It's for the whole world to see, Alabama snow, won't be back for a while.

My Soul Floats

My soul floats down, never to part from my God. Just like an eagle that glides through the beautiful blue sky. I'm relaxed as I can be and light as a feather, I am very happy in this place, to be. My soul floats down to a beautiful place you see, to connect with my God.

I was taken to the next level in the middle of the sky. I am on a bed of white clouds as peaceful as I can be. In this place, I had no pain. I was glad to be there in such a beautiful place. I was amazed to be there. My soul floats down, I'm as happy as I can be. I'm in a long white gown, picking beautiful flowers. Walking through a rose garden. As I looked around to see where I was, I heard this voice that whispered to me. Go back my child, I am not ready for you. It is not your time to be with me. My soul floats down, I could not see the face of this person, that was speaking to me, for it was so cloudy there. I looked around to find myself awakening in the emergency room. I asked the doctors why did you wake me up. I had a beautiful, peaceful, lovely dream. The doctors looked at me and said, "you were legally dead you were not dreaming. We had to resuscitate you". God, has given me a second time to change my life around, as my soul floats down. It is a feeling you will never, ever forget; when your soul floats down.

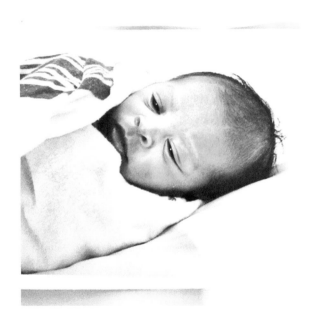

Granny's Little Man

Granny's little man was born crying. I thank God for my little man. Granny's little man's first word was "hey", we were surprised to hear a baby say hey at three days old. I love my little man. Granny's little man will make you smile, that will take your breath away.

Granny's little man was born just to make granny happy, and cheerful once again.

Find Love

Until your cares have passed away, be assured that love,
will bring you joy and happiness that last a lifetime. God's
love will never let you fall. God's love will never grow old.
God's love can never be bought or stolen. When you find
God's love, that is the greatest love of all.

Choose God's love, and then God will choose you. God will
never let you part, you will always be in his heart.

King James Version (KJV)
1. John 4:8 He that loveth not knoweth not God; for God is love.

Nosey Neighbors

I am your nosy neighbor. I sit on my porch to watch you come and go. I talk on the phone so I can see what I can talk about some more., I gossip about things I know, and that I don't know. I know your income; I know who you are dating. I know when you take a bath, I know when you are sleeping, I know what you are eating. I know when you are sick, I can tell the time the nurses arrive at your door, I know when they leave. When I am home alone, I leave my home and go down the street, to see what's going on I am a nosey neighbor. I have nothing to do but be in your business because I like garbage. I can tell you what time you leave home and when you come back home. I am a nosey neighbor, it's my job to be in your business because I am the nosy neighbor. I talked about the rich and the poor; the young and the old; the fat, and the skinny; the good, and the bad; pretty and the ugly. I'm a nosey neighbor and I do not care. you cannot stop me because I am a nosey neighbor. Will you please join me?

King James Version (KJV)
Proverbs 21:23 Whoso keepeth his mouth and tongue keepeth his soul from trouble.

Mind

My mind wandered for hours from place to place it went. I could feel my body being worn out; my soul was being lifted out of me slowly, and slowly it goes. I stopped to think about God, have I failed him. Suddenly I stop to think about God's grace and mercy.

Where this life is taking me, am I on a runway to heaven or the runway to hell? Where is this life taking me what is this what could this be? Why am I tormented, where am I going? Certainly, my mind, speaks to my body with breath and affirmation of divinity.

It's time for a different system. Committing to myself to treat it with care and love. To create a holey temple. To sing for God, it eases my pain; to praise his holey name.

The Devil Can't Stop God's Blessing

That old devil keeps stirring up trouble each day. Every time we turn, around that old devil, is standing right in our way. The devil comes to us in different shapes. Some people are like the devil, eases upon you, and is the biggest devil in the world. The devil can't learn your profile; they get jealous and start rumors and lies. God blesses us each day. God's blessing is for a lifetime. Tell that old devil to get out of the way!

Smile

Smile because you are happy. Smile because you are not in pain. Smile because you are not insane, you have a sound mind. Smile because you have no money, it will come another day. Smile because you are not alone. God is in love with you. Smile because you can walk with Jesus. That is the only way to go.

King James Version (KJV)
Proverbs 17:22 A merry heart doeth good like a medicine: but a broken spirit drieth the bones.

The Day I Received My Wings

One night I dreamed I was a beautiful white dove. I was flying to the sky to reach the stars. I had long white beautiful wings, that an angel gave to me, to protect me from the cold. I went into the light; a voice spoke to me; "my child you have no fear here." I went through the shadow of darkness, as I traveled through a voice said to come with me, my child. I am with you all the way you have nothing to fear here. Here everything looked so strange. I went to this beautiful city that was so glittery, such as shiny gold. I was not afraid! From there, I went to the heavenly land. I fell to my knees for it was God's heavenly home, my soul had traveled home. For this was peace for me. To see my God's heavenly throne... An angel came to me where I received my robe and crown. The robe was draped upon my shoulders. The crown was placed upon my head. I was given such beautiful golden shoes. To walk the golden streets. The angel escorted me to my new heavenly home through the pearly gates. A mansion with no pain or stress. Only peace, happiness, and love. There was dancing and praising God everywhere. I have won the victory at last. I can smile once

again. The day I received my wings. Do God's will and live
right you can see this heavenly place too.

King James Version (KJV)
John 14:1-3

1. Let not your heart be troubled: ye believe in God, believe also in me.

2. In my Father's house are many mansions: if it were not so, I would have told you. I go to prepare a place for you.

3. And if I go and prepare a place for you, I will come again, and receive you unto myself; that where I am, there ye may be also.

My Favorite Child

*My favorite child is at my side if I am lonely, sad,
depressed, in pain. My strength, my guide, my inspira-
tion my courage. My favorite child never lets me down.
Comforts me when I am in need and makes me smile.
My favorite child is irreplaceable. I was blessed the day
my favorite child was born. No one can take the place of
my favorite child. I was blessed the day God gave me my
favorite child.*

Call Your Mother

The day you were born I was so glad to see your little beautiful face. Oh, what joy you bought to me. I was there for you through your trials and tribulation. I held your hand when you were sick, through good times and bad. I gave you food to eat, put clothes on your back. Now you are all grown up and gone away. I pray daily for you. I wish you all well and this old world that's filled with sorrow, lies, tears, and pain. Call your mother yesterday, has come and gone away. I'm still sitting here waiting and rocking in this old rocking chair. Looking out this window. Just to hear your voice with a sweet hello. The years have come and gone away. Now I am old, wrinkle, and gray. Waiting on just one to call with a sweet hello. Stop and call your mother, OH this is no way to be. I have given you so many toys and things when you were little. We never missed one happy holiday that was filled with joy and cheer. Maybe I have given you too much in the world. Now you're all grown up and gone away. You never come by or call with a sweet hello. Call your mother, oh what could this be that you will stay away from me. As I wipe the tears that fall, from my eyes down on my face. These tears that, I cry just to see your face to be by your side, or hear a sweet hello. Do not deny your mother, whether she is black or white, old or young, fat or skinny, ugly, or pretty, do not be ashamed of your mother. So many people have mothers that have left this world. Now they only wish they could hear her voice. Do not wait until it is too late to call your mother before time sits still. That is your mother just because she is black or white, old or young, pretty or ugly, fat or skinny. That is your mother. Stop. Call your mother before time sits still. Would you recognize me I am old, wrinkled, and gray? Stop! Call your mother don't deny your mother.

King James Version (KJV)

1 Timothy 5:4 But if any widow have children or nephews, let them learn first to show piety at home, and to requite their parents: for that is good and acceptable before God.

A Child's Fears

I want to call my mother. I forgot to call my mother when I became rich and famous. I forgot to call my mother. I wonder if she is okay now that my eyes grow dim, every year that comes to an end. I find myself all grown up wrinkle and gray. I forgot to pray for my mother where is she now. I forgot about my mother when I became rich and proud. Now I am filled with tears, as I called my mother, just to say hello. I wonder will mother welcome me now, that I am old and gray. I want to see my mother, one more time.

Mother Wish

As I sit in my corner looking out the window. I wish my
child will come home; The Lord restores my heart it is
oh so empty, my hope rise and fall with each setting sun
for reasons unknown. Suddenly! I hear this soft voice say
mother I am home. God's loveliness is all around me that
my child has come home.

Stuck In Neutral

I'm stuck in neutral I'm going nowhere. I'm stuck in neutral and I don't care. I repeat the same thing each day; why?

Because I'm stuck in neutral! I'm going nowhere. I don't want to work I just beg for your money and you give it to me.

I'm stuck in neutral I don't care. I don't need or want a job.

I'm used to begging for money and letting you take care of me, as long as you give me your money, I will take it.

I'm stuck in neutral I don't care; I will come and beg you for your clothes and you give them to me because I'm stuck in neutral

I'm going nowhere. I'm stuck in neutral and I don't care.

Why Lie

*Why lie because you can? When you lie that lie will grow.
Why lie because you are all alone, have no friends? It is not
a lie to you.*

*Why lie because you are angry, at the world? Why lie
because you have no money or no big house? Get up and
get a job, and have self -preservation.*

King James Version (KJV)
Psalm Chapter 101:7 He that worketh deceit shall not dwell within
my house; he that telleth lies shall not tarry in my sight.

As We Transform

The day we conceive we transform, developed, into an embryo then a fetus. Unborn baby to a newborn baby as we transform.

We started to sit alone; we crawled took our first steps. We started to walk, to run, from a baby to a young child, an adult life cycle to an older person. Into the painful body that we do not want. As we transform back to God, our work on earth is done.

King James Version (KJV)
Romans 12:2 And be not conformed to this world: but be ye transformed by the renewing of your mind, that ye may prove what is that good, and acceptable, and perfect, will of God.

Paradise

Paradise is a beautiful place with water from the deep blue sea. Which flows from the ocean floor.

Down from a waterfall on a rocky mountain. That flows into a stream, filled with lily flowers.

Paradise is a beautiful place for you and me to see, a joyful, lovely place that has no sin or shame.

As we're walking through paradise one last time where time sits still, escape from everyone.

Paradise was made for both you and me.

As we walked through paradise filled with peace, with beautiful flowers that would take your breath away, the scent of roses, jasmine, and sweet pea flowers that blows through a soft windy breeze, safe and free; paradise was made for both you and me. Just to be free in paradise will take your breath away.

God's Gift

God, blessed you with this perfect gift. The sacred gift of Christmas can't be bought or sold.

God's love is Brighter than pure gold, it can't be found in any store, or wrapped beneath a Christmas tree. The day Jesus was born was sweeter than anything in the world. The most important gift is that God has given you, his Son.

With Joy, peace, love, and happiness may all the best gifts of Christmas be yours always! Have a cheerful wonderful and happy new year in Christian love this year.

King James Version (KJV)
James 1:17 Every good gift and every perfect gift is from above, and cometh down from the Father of lights, with whom is no variableness, neither shadow of turning.

If Tomorrow Never Comes

*If tomorrow never comes; Gods' gates have opened wide;
You walked right on the inside; your work on earth is done.
You had a race to run. Now it's finished; The road was
long and hard; so many mountains you had to climb. You
fought a good fight and you have finally won the victory.
It's okay. You are no longer hurting. Now your battle on
earth is done. You have finished the course.*

*God took you by the hand and led you right inside. I am
trying not to cry, it is so hard to say goodbye, but your good
memories and love will last a lifetime; You are a guardian
angel now and I know you are smiling down. If tomorrow
never comes.*

Letter To Mother

Out of all the entire women in this whole wide world. Our God has chosen you to give us birth. We are filled with happiness and joy, one day everything will be better. That we will see your face again, on the other side of heaven. There's nothing in this world that can keep us from loving you when you were here. We miss you, mamma. Mamma, we want you to know that no matter how hard things may seem now, to us. Through the trials and tribulations, we have in life. There's always gold at the end of the rainbow. Mamma no matter what we want you to know we are keeping our heads up. We are keeping our faith in God to bring us through. All the things that have been happening here on this earth. There is nothing that we can do, but keep our eyes on the prize that is God. mamma, we love you and miss you so much.

Hope In Tomorrow

*Have hope in tomorrow, is not pretending that there's
never any sorrow. It's the knowledge that our troubles, will
be overcome tomorrow. It's the inner strength we call on
now and then. Till our problems are beneath us, will have
a chance tomorrow. and we're happy once again. It's not
looking back for yesterday. That day is gone away never
to return, so put your faith in God, he is the one, the only
one. May you find hope and inner peace, till all your cares
have passed away, and says to come will bring you joy,
peace, love, and happiness that last a lifetime. There is hope
in tomorrow.*

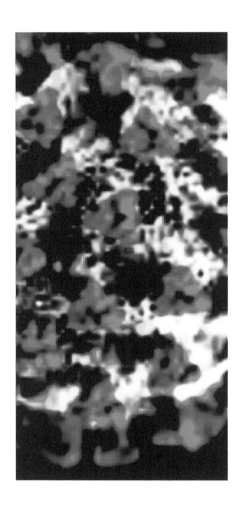

Coronavirus / Covid 19

COVID 19 traveled around the world, by eyes unseen. Invisible, unknown to anyone. It travels state by state quickly.

It does not discriminate. COVID 19, visited many people young and old. It comes to make you sick and in pain. It will take your life away. COVID 19 made our stores close down, don't let your guard down. It will be here to hang around. Wash your hands, wear your mask. Keep your distance, it will sneak up on you. COVID 19 will soon be long gone only a memory, in history. Do not take, it for granted, this is a dangerous virus.

My Loving Sister

So many times, I've thanked God for giving me a wonderful sister like you. I love you for helping me safe, across life's highways. If you were not there, oh I would have let go. your love has done more for me than silver and gold. If you were a big beautiful butterfly. You would spread your wings out and never let me fall. No one knows what exactly you mean to me it could not be put into words. You listen and gave me, the wisdom that I needed and did not judge me. I am glad that we can share so many interesting things in this world together that we love. Especially our faith, God's love is so real for me, and you're understanding too. Your concern has always meant so much. So many thoughtful things you have done have made me understand. You did it without a grumbling word. That's why I'm thanking God for the blessing of you being my sister. I am praying that God, will always keep us in His loving care. My dearest sister, I love you so much.

One Day At A Time

One day at a time whether the goals we're pursuing. This life will never be perfect, no matter how rugged the mountains we climb.

We're certain to get there by trying our best and taking one day at a time. "Forever " is hard to imagine, what the future holes.

We cannot see in the future " it is so far away. But every new loving day brings a wonderful challenge in life, a chance to do what we can on that day. As you reach for the goals you would like to achieve. May you find all the strength you will need, to meet every challenge one step at a time till the day when you proudly succeed. One day at a time.

Broken

The whole world I carry on my back, everyone turns against me at my weakest point I am broken. I looked around no one to console me., I am so sad my heart seems as if a thorn has pierced my heart; I am broken. I have traveled a long road alone. I see things so clearly. I have mountains to climb, obstacles in my way. My heart filled with pain as I walked alone. I was drawn to the sea, which chilled my mind, soul, and body, it was so cold. All alone walking from one end of the ocean floor to the other that knows, no time. I want to be alone, with no one to seek me. I am here to clear and cleanse my mind I am broken. As I prayed and prayed, I grew stronger. God gave me strength. God sent his angel to secure my broken heart, rapping me with love. God held my hand and made me smile again. If you can't smile, just remember that God holds the key to death, Heaven, and Hell. That will make you smile again. I truly thank God for showing me the way as I run this race. It doesn't matter what you've been through in life. It is whatever you are doing that is good in this world. We must stay prayed up as we make our journey on our way home to our heavenly father.

Different Degrees Of Love

Different degrees of love I love you but I'm not in love with you. I love you a little. I love you less I love myself and no one else. I love you for who you are. Some love to be loved, some love for money. Some love more than others. Some love to be rich. Some love their bachelor's degrees. Some love their nursing degree. Some love people. Doctors love to take care of sick people, that is why they have their doctor's degrees. Some people love earthly things. It is many different degrees of love in this world. Love is an internal thing. Don't get generosity too confused with love. Just because someone is generous, it does not mean a person is in love with you.

Don't get love confused with kindness. There is no love greater than God's love.

King James Version (KJV)
John 3:16 For God so loved the world, that he gave his only begotten Son, that whoever believeth in him should not perish, but have everlasting life.

Invigorating Mind

A tear of fear to, let go. Making one's revolution around the world as the sun revolves. In a state of nature; I was no longer hidden now; to go fulfill my destiny. Feeling that you've done something wrong. I find myself slowly liberated; I no longer have a problem with standing out. As I discover myself. What good is destiny if you're not healthy enough to walk that path? I know why God has granted me a female warrior tribe. It sank in so many areas of my being. I, feel intense or passionate dislike. No longer will I let anyone abuse or take me for granted. When they say, Get out of your way, it's a surprising and previously unknown fact. I have escaped; I was chained and bound; I have broken the chains. I am no longer chained or bound. It is time for a complete renovation and no boundaries. With an appreciation, I have the quality of being coherent and intelligent. I make better decisions to grow in this world. For my work I must, achieve all successful solutions. It is time for a complete renovation. Stripping myself, of secrets Insecurities, and lack of confidence. With, an appreciation I have the quality of being coherent and intelligent. I make better decisions to grow for my work ahead. I welcome this new, heart and invigorating mind.

Cotton-Picking Time

This old truck rolls around each day, for Big Mamma it is Cotton Picking time. Big Mamma must be on time at the break of dawn as this old truck rolled around it is Cotton Picking time. Everyone climbs on the back of this truck, Big Mamma arrived in the field at about 6 a.m. Big mamma had to feed the family that day. She had to make it work, it was Cotton Picking time. Big Mamma would pick 300 or 400 pounds of cotton a day. She would never take a break. The children took a break, it would be orange aid, boloney, crackers, cheese, or can sardines. Big Mamma was hungry, hot, thirsty, and tired. Big Mamma works in the field all day long.

This long Sack filled it with cotton. The sack straps around her shoulder to her back. She would be dragging it behind her in the fields. When we would look up big mamma was the only one, halfway at the end of the row. She was picking more than one row at a time. It was Cotton Picking time. At the end of the day, big mamma was paid such little money for the hard work she did. Big mamma had enough money to feed the family for that day. They would call the boss, boss-man this made him proud. Boss-man was stopped at this little General Store. So, his workers could get the food they needed that day for the family.

Boss- man-made Shure the workers spend their money.
To return to the fields the next day because it was cotton-
picking time. Big Mamma picked up food for the family at
the end of the day. The next day was the same, for it was
Cotton Picking time. Big Mamma did her best, she was
a heart working woman. Just to keep food on the table
for her family it was Cotton-Picking time. Big Mamma
was happy just to see the children eat with a smile on
their faces.

The Paine

The pain is trying to steal your life away. The pain will try to steal your mind, your body, and your soul away if you let it be. This sickness lies deep down in your soul, your mind, and your body. It will take your life away only if you let it be. I am all alone at night this pain won't let me be, as my face turns red.; As flames and the fire this pain won't let me be. As I toss and turn all night oh what can it be, doctors can't find out. What's wrong with me, will you please let me be? This Pain will drive you insane, will you let me be. The pain that has known no, boundaries' you will never see. Deep down in my soul; would you please let me be. Is this the end for me oh Lord please oh Lord please don't let it be the end for me? Jesus bears the pain to save souls like me.

King James Version (KJV)
Revelation 21:4 And God shall wipe away all tears from their eyes; and there shall be no more death, neither sorrow, nor crying, neither shall there be any more pain: for the former things are passed away.

Shack Avenue

On Shack Avenue, A true story in Alabama was a difficult time in life. This young girl married a man at the age of eleven years old, the husband was thirty years old. The marriage was arranged by her father. She was given to this older man thinking she would have a better life. Her first child was born at the age of twelve. Soon after she said he was acting as her father instead of a husband, he was very cantankerous. She had to do everything he said as if she were a child. His instructions were carried out with precision.

Each year she would have a baby, a total of twenty-one children on shack avenue. The husband and his wife agreed to have this large family, as the children would grow up to help them make money. They lived on this farm rent-free in exchange for work on the farmland, they were sharecroppers. Her fourth child was only three months old when the baby, died in the mother's arms. From undernourished and lacked the care the baby needed from the mother. She worked long hours for which she made one dollar per day.

She thought this was a good job, for the money she made in a day. Washing, ironing, cleaning, cooking, scrubbing the floor on her hands and knees were her usual duties.

She was glad for the money but sorry she lost her baby.
She did not weep very much because she was pregnant
again. Down on shack avenue, the seven-year-old would
sit and scream all day. It was discovered that he had a
brain tumor that caused his demise. Now he can take his
rest. He is at peace at last, on shack Avenue. In this little
house, on a dirt road on a dead-end street. They were poor
in this rural area down south way back in the country,
miles away from anyone. On shack avenue, there were two
bedrooms and nineteen siblings. Their father noticed the
house was overcrowded. The father turned their back porch
into a bedroom for the boys which they called a boy's room.
During Christmas time was a great celebration, with more
food than they had all year. The children would catch opos-
sums, to be cooked with baked sweet potatoes. Christmas
day, their boss-man would come bearing gifts with a big
box of hand-me-down clothes, for the children along with
apples, oranges, peppermint candy, and chocolate cake.
They made their toys, a make-believe horse from a broom-
stick and toys made of wire. The older girls could make
paper dolls and dresses for the little girls. They enjoyed
family time together. They had a radio for entertainment
later in the day. Their mother said she enjoyed being
pregnant. She said the pain did not bother her. She said the
bible said, "multiply."

Later that day, her son saw her go across the field. He said"
yonder she goes," When she returned, she had a baby in
her arms.

He did not understand where the baby came from.
This confused the little boy. But it was another joyful
Christmas gift.

A new sister on Christmas day. They had no electricity for
lights to see at night, only oil lamps to light their way. Their
father used oil lamps on the wagon and mule at night. No
running water, only a well to pull water from, with tin
buckets to hold the water on Shack Avenue. In the rainy
season, their roof would leak. They had to put buckets on
the floor to catch the rain that leaked from their ceiling.

The rainwater they caught, was saved for washing clothes,
taking a bath, and animals to drink. No central heat or
air, only a fireplace to keep them warm in the wintertime
on Shack Avenue. They had a little cast iron stove, with
a cast-iron kettle to heat water., a solid fuel such as wood
or coal burned to produce heat for warmth and cooking.
The son said, "They had a washing machine and a dryer
that turned out; To be a round tin tub with a rub-board."
Wash day was on Saturday, all the girls did the washing.
The drier was a homemade clothesline to dry their clothes.
They made soap which was called lye soap. At dinner
time chickens were killed just for dinner. They had so
little food, some children had to go without; especially the
children that refused the chicken heads and feet. In the
Summertime, the heat was so hot they could hardly bear
it. They would leave the windows up just to get a breeze of
air. The mosquitoes were glad because it was their dinner
time. The children made themselves a fan from cardboard
boxes just to beat the mosquitos off on Shack Avenue. The
bathroom was outside, down a hill in the woods. It was

called an outhouse. In the wintertime, it was so cold. The children said it seems their bodies would freeze while going to the outhouse. They were afraid to go outside at night. Because this place was in a desolate area. The wild animals were too numerous for them. The wild animals would run and play, on Shack Avenue. They had corn shuck and hay mattresses Which were shared with the rats, roaches, and bugs. Their entertainment was to go to church on Sunday and Wednesday for prayer service. Emotions were o so difficult to bear on Shack Avenue. Their father had a car that he called a Cadillac. That car was a wagon and a mule until he upgraded to a bike. Before the older children went to school, they had to be up at sunrise, to milk the cows feed the hogs, goats, and chickens. After school, they had to chop the wood and pick the cotton. The money from the cotton was not enough to feed the family. The father noticed the girls were coming up pregnant; they were forbidden to have a boyfriend. Their father was determined to find out who was the father of the girl's pregnancy. So, he waited until the babies were born. Then he pulled his belt off and threatened to beat each one. He found out the boys and girls had committed an abomination. They were having babies with their brothers. They were never to speak about this deadly sin or say anything to anyone as long as, he lived. Their father thought he had failed in life. Their father was angry, he made the older boys go into the military, he thought they would learn discipline. He decided that the girls leave home and find jobs. The grandchildren stayed with their grandparents. The daughters sent money back home to help take care of their children. Their father *was so disgusted with his children, this weighed heavily on his mind. He was so heartbroken, that he thought he had made an error in raising them. By being involved in the church and a Christian, their father forgave his children for their sins. Burdens and emotions were so difficult in this little house. One thing this little house had that no other house had. It had a lot, of fatherly love down on Shack Avenue.*

Aging

We were living in Port Charles, New Zealand. With all my children, they grew up so fast. With each generation's grandchildren, thereafter Soon to be my loving great-grand. This is the love of life to see, all my children. From these roots, four generations were born. My body is stricken with such difficult pain. The brighter day was when we were young and had no pain. We went to the doctors; the doctors said to take a family vacation, to release the stress, we were getting older. My husband made me a bright promise that we can travel around the world before we are too old. I slowly turned looked at my husband he forgot we were old.

Making me this bright promise, and his hair was divorcing his head. It looked like a hot mess when your hair run away from your head.

He said he will get a toupee in gray he bought one in red. We went to Texas we were bold and the beautiful, when we were young. I thought we were young and restless until I looked in the mirror, the wrinkles look like, sprinkles.

We were on top of the world love is a many splendored things. When you are young and happy now, we are old and snappy.

We went to New York the city, we visit the Capitol in Albany County. We took the ferry to liberty island. To see, the statue of liberty.

When we arrived, we were tired then we had to tinkle, as soon as we had seen a fountain sprinkle. now we are aging. We went to visit, Sunset Beach; it is a seaside town in Brunswick County, North Carolina. We set down to watch the sunset we forgot our age; we went to sleep because we were not the young and the restless, we were old and bold. When we woke up it was a new day; with the bright rising sun, right into the guiding light of the day. We went to visit Somerset it is a Country, in South West England a beautiful place.

The Somerset village of Cheddar is the home of the famous cheese. We do not eat cheese since we are aging. This was the love of life traveling, we have seen so many beautiful places and things. My family has a passion for traveling; around the world. The brighter day has passed us by; the years have come and gone away now we are aging. We were in shape when we were young now, we sit and shake. Now we have lost our sense, of smell and taste, we are aging. No longer can we see as we search for tomorrow; we ended up with dark shadows under our eyes. We started to lose, our sight as we are aging. My knees started to crack since my back had an attack. The pain drives you insane since we can't ascertain, we are in, the secret storm. No longer we are; the bold and the beautiful. We have false teeth since our teeth fell out, our mussels went flat and we got fat. Now we are aging. Now here comes gout.

We have one life to live; as the world turns. These are the days of our lives as we grow old. Since we appear, we can't hear now, we have no cheer we are aging. Here comes dementia to put us in another world. We are stuck in the twilight zone. Now we are ending up in the general hospital now that we are aging. We wanted to visit Ryan's Hope my husband's cousin. He lives in Estonia it is a country on the eastern coast of the Baltic Sea in Northern Europe. Too long to travel. Home is where the heart is, we are ready to go home. No more traveling for us, only a rocking chair it will be. It is no longer a destiny; it's a journey now; that we are aging.

Roses Beneath My Wings

Roses beneath my wings; the day I left you, I wanted to be with you all. In a fraction of a second, God called my name and I had to leave. It was my time to go, to be with God. Life will be difficult now that I am known longer there. Remember God will take care of you. Try your best to keep up your spirit. I'm sorry I can't hug, kiss, and touch your beautiful faces. Remember you are my roses beneath my wings. I hear your cries. I see the tears and the pain. I am so far away like a glittering, star in the sky. I hear you call my name. I can't answer you. You are My roses beneath my wings. Even though you can't see me. I am here for you. I can reach out and spread my wings around you, rapping you in my love. I love you all so smile for me. My lovely roses beneath my wings.

Acknowledgment

Giving all the praise, honor, and glory to my God without God, I would never make it. If it wasn't for him, I wouldn't be where I am today. To my family thank you for your support. Thank God for the crown of righteousness, also to all who have longed for his appearance.

Evangelist Rodney Comer for giving me the support that I needed. Telling me to never give up and stop listening to any critics. Through my pain tears, and heartaches. Thank you for your prayers and motivation.

Dedicated to Lillie Jackson who encourages me to write so many years ago. Even though you are no longer here. Your faith in God your prayers, love, and your encouragement have made me strong. Rest in peace; mother.

Advance praise

"Elizabeth Billups has experienced rock bottom in life. The reason for writing this book is to let people know you are not alone when it comes to pain. Now she has a story to tell that is cautionary and uplifting. It is worth reading."

Sargent
Justin Billups (son)

"Elizabeth Billups Her story is a vivid one to anyone facing similar pain. This book has powerful feelings. I admire your strength you are a woman full of knowledge. You are my inspiration; I love you."

Motivational speaker
Jason Billups (son)

Printed in the USA
CPSIA information can be obtained
at www.ICGtesting.com
LVHW071750190424
777896LV00026B/294